BRICKWORK FOR BEGINNERS

GARDEN MATTERS

BRICKWORK FOR BEGINNERS

STEWART FRASER

WARD LOCK

First published in Great Britain in 1991
by Ward Lock Limited, Villiers House,
41/47 Strand, London WC2N 5JE, England

A Cassell Imprint

© Ward Lock Limited

Line drawings by Mike Shoebridge

Text filmset in 11/11½ point ITC Garamond Light
by Columns of Reading
Printed and bound in Great Britain by
Collins Manufacturing, Glasgow

British Library Cataloguing in Publication Data

Fraser, Stewart
Brickwork for beginners. – (Garden matters)
1. Gardens
I. Title   II. Series
712.6

ISBN 0–7063–7026–0

CONTENTS

PREFACE

Houses and gardens go together: they are complementary. Brick is a well established material for both buildings and the garden. Most of us come to a house, and a garden, that has already been created. We may want to make changes, but hesitate. We lack experience and know-how.

This book will show you how to use brickwork, in a variety of ways, to enhance the garden. Projects are provided which are simple and straightforward, progressing carefully to more adventurous ideas. There is an indication of the varieties of brick available, in finish, colour, and shape. The text shows how brick can stand on its own, or live with a variety of other materials. Information and advice, in words and illustrations, is provided in full; there is no assumption of any prior knowledge or ability. Hence it is very much a book for beginners who want to learn.

This is a necessary publication for all those who want to improve their home environment, within the resources available of money, time and expertise. Anyone who follows the progressive system in this book will soon learn how to make the most of the opportunities available, to make house and garden something of beauty, and of pleasure.

S.F.

INTRODUCTION

A house and a garden form two parts of one environment – the home. This environment is a place of relaxation, where the family can enjoy being together.

In many cases, the house will be built in brick. And brick becomes a sensible item for work in the garden. In other cases, brick is still a suitable material, simply because it is so natural and friendly. It blends in with most styles of housing, most materials. The one problem, for the beginner, is just how to go about using this sympathetic material, to the best advantage.

It's perhaps worth recalling that brick-making is one of the oldest crafts around. It goes right back, several thousands of years. We have a long heritage behind us. Nowadays, we don't make our own bricks, but archaeologists tell us that Neolithic man did his own thing. He used clay from the earth to make pottery. And he used it to make bricks. The first ones were probably simply shaped by hand, and left to bake in the sun. People soon took up this idea.

There was the problem that buildings made of earth, mud as it were, tended to disappear after heavy rainfall. Clay was better, and clay that had dried out properly was well worth the effort.

By the time the people of Jericho were looking to make a wall round their city, the technique was to use a mould for the bricks. People in Egypt needed straw to bind it: those in Jericho didn't.

In places like Babylon there were some highly talented workers. Bricks were fired, and glazed. Palaces had all sorts of decorative work – lions, bulls, winged beasts. All a few thousand years ago.

It was, inevitably, the Romans who introduced brickwork to Britain. The local climate meant that fired bricks were necessary. Mud and rain never did mix. The idea of using second-hand bricks gained in popularity once the Romans left for home. Old buildings were knocked down and used for Norman and Saxon structures.

Elsewhere in Europe, in contrast, new brickwork was popular for great cathedrals in the Gothic style. And in America, there were many examples of Tudor-style houses – lots of bricks, and often lots of wood as well.

BRICKS, BRICKS, BRICKS

Yet bricks seem to have an appeal all of their own. They come in a vast range of sizes, colours, textures, and strengths. It is something of a specialist field, in fact.

Essentially, there are two kinds of clay bricks to consider. There are the common or building bricks, and there are the facing bricks. Ordinary building bricks are used for general work, where appearance is not of special significance. Strength is still important, and so is the ability to stand up to the vagaries of weather. Facing bricks, as the name suggests, are used for a particular appearance. They come in different strengths. Some are red, blue, purple, yellow, brown or grey. Some have a mixture of colours. They can be smooth, textured by machine, or include sand on the outside face.

Different countries give different names to classifications of quality. Essentially, however, what it comes to is bricks are divided into those that will do only for work inside a building; others which cover the vast range of ordinary work required; and a few others which are more suitable for extreme conditions.

Shapes, again, certainly do vary. Some of the names used include single bullnose (one end curved), double bullnose (two ends curved), plinth header (with a slope at one end), cant brick (much the same), double cant (two ends sloping in), and plinth stretcher (with a slope, but a wider brick).

And just to complete the picture, there are different sizes of bricks. One 'standard' size is 215 mm × 102.5 mm × 65 mm. There has to be allowance for mortar, to hold the bricks together. That means adding 10 mm for the mortar joint. So your standard brick is known as a nominal 225 mm × 112.5 mm × 75 mm.

For the imperialists, bricks are $8\frac{5}{8}$ in × $4\frac{1}{8}$ in × $2\frac{5}{8}$ in. Taking $\frac{3}{8}$ in for joints, the nominal size becomes 9 in × $4\frac{1}{2}$ in × 3 in. These nominal sizes are the ones used in measuring, to give the number of bricks for a given length, or height.

There is no reason to be deterred by all this. Any craft is going to have its own special language, or jargon. Lots of things will be strange and unfamiliar. But you really don't need more than a passing look at fancy names and shapes. What you do is look at the actual bricks available from your local merchant.

We're talking about ordinary bricks, suitable for work in the garden. They should be all the same size and shape. All the same material, and for this stage of work, all the same colour and texture. Don't be afraid to ask. Ask if the bricks really are suitable for work in the garden. Make sure they are not for inside work: that is important. Ask what size they are. If the man gives a figure in millimetres, you have gone metric, like it or not. Otherwise, you are still in the old-style feet and inches.

What happens, you may ask, if you don't want to buy new materials, but have the chance to use second-hand bricks? Well, that's easy, too. Ask the person selling the goods – what size are these bricks? Or just measure them, and see what size you have.

The only effective difference is that you will be either talking about building 'four courses to a foot' – the old term in brickwork for the height of four rows of bricks – or you're talking about 'four courses to 300 mm'. Four courses, to a nominal height of 3 in or 75 mm each. They're really the same thing.

It will, of course, make sense to try to standardize on your material. If an existing wall, say, was made in 9-in bricks, look for similar ones to do any repairs or additions. It keeps the courses level.

Now that we have reassured ourselves that brickwork really can be simple and straightforward, let's move on a bit.

TERMINOLOGY

We'll need to know some terms, and we'll need to consider suitable tools for our work.

Terminology first. As already indicated, bricks are laid in rows, which are known as courses. A brick used lengthways is called a stretcher, and one used across its width is a header.

If you are building a wall, the way to make sure it does not fall down is to have the rows of bricks overlapping at the joints, making a bond. You can make pleasant patterns as well as ensuring the survival of your work by using the bricks this way. Figure 1 shows how a wall with bricks in straight lines is not as strong as one where lines are staggered. The bond spreads the load effectively. It is, incidentally, a stretcher bond: more of that later.

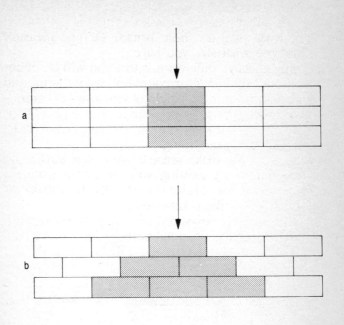

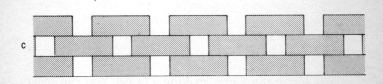

FIG. 1 *Brick bonds* (a) *No bond – no strength. A load would go straight down.* (b) *A good bond – spreads the load. This one is stretcher bond.* (c) *This is known as open bond – a gap of up to 75 mm (3 in) between bricks.*

Terms we will need are half-brick, or half bat, meaning a brick cut in half across its length. If we have bricks joined end to end, and a course above that with an overlap on the joints, then we leave a 'half' space somewhere. We need to have some cut bricks in our pattern to even things out. There are also three-quarter bricks in some bonds.

A possible confusion is when you have a half-brick wall. That is not one made of broken pieces – just bricks laid end to end. The bricks run lengthwise, which means the width of the wall is the width of a brick. The width is half its length. Hence the half-brick name.

Figure 1 shows a bit about bonds. For a start, no bond means no strength. A proper bond means good strength. Then there is stretcher bond, for a half-brick wall. Notice the shape at the corner, and how the bricks overlap. The drawing also shows what an open bond looks like – stretcher bond, but with a gap between bricks, about 75 mm (3 in) and slightly less at the corner.

Once you start taking an interest in brickwork, you will see for yourself how houses, walls, paths or drives all use bonds and patterns. You will notice how the builder turns corners or gives extra strength with piers as needed.

Mortar is the mixture that keeps the bricks together, and concrete is the stronger mixture that makes, for example, foundations for walls. Buttering is placing the mortar on the bricks. Pointing is dealing with the joints, to finish off your work.

With tools there is no particular confusion. A problem of which ones to buy, perhaps. But that can always be decided on straightforward grounds.

EQUIPMENT

What do you really need? That's the basic question.

Something to make sure you work on the level. Something to make sure your courses (rows of bricks) are also level, and straight up and down. Something to make your mortar or concrete. Something to put it on the bricks, or into the foundations.

You are probably not going to take up bricklaying as a full-time job. You don't particularly want to spend more than you have to. Figure 2 shows some basic equipment. Add more later if you wish.

A *trowel* – a 25 cm (10 in) blade – is fine for the mortar, but it's not suitable for cutting bricks. For that purpose, a *bolster* is well worthwhile. This is a form of chisel, with a wide metal blade. It is struck with, usually, a *club hammer*. This has a fairly short handle and a heavy head, just right for use with a chisel.

Keeping things even is not difficult: use an ordinary *spirit level* (one with 'bubbles' to check both horizontal and vertical is handy). Making sure your courses are straight also means having something long and level. A line of *string* that won't stretch, and some means of holding the two ends tight, is what you use.

For the rest, a *spotboard* on which to mix the mortar is just that, a board about 60 cm (2 ft) square. Concrete will need a larger mixing area: a *tarpaulin or sheet of plastic, or a piece of hardboard*.

A *hawk* is the name for a smaller square of plywood – 23 cm (9 in) will do – with a piece of an old broom for a handle. This holds small amounts of mortar for working with bricks. A *float* smooths down concrete and is a piece of flat wood – sometimes a piece of metal – with a handle.

A strong *bucket or pail* is used for measuring and carrying materials. A *spade or shovel* gets the materials

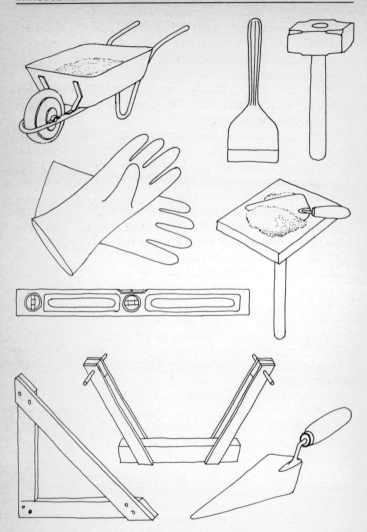

FIG. 2 *A selection of some equipment you may use: barrow, bolster and club hammer, gloves, hawk, spirit level, 3:4:5 square, one form of tamper, and trowel.*

together. *Gloves* keep your hands in proper order – an important point this – and *old clothes and shoes* are also likely to be insisted upon by certain members of the family.

Other items are handy. Some you can make for yourself, and details will be given as we progress through our projects.

How do you make sure corners are square to begin with? How do you know your courses are rising the same distance each time? How do you ensure bats are the right size, every time? Does concrete level itself out, or can you help the process?

To re-state the situation. We are going to learn the basics of brickwork. We're not pretending to be full-time professionals, but we'll know what we're doing and how best to go about it.

We don't want to spend a fortune, but no-one said we couldn't borrow from a friend or neighbour. No-one said we couldn't hire pieces of equipment from a local garden centre. And we're not out to create any records for speeding along.

With any kind of work, the secret of success – if there is a secret – is simply to take it carefully. Work things out in your mind; have a dry run with the materials. Have a go with spare pieces – try cutting an old, bashed-about brick before you go on to brand-new ones. Decide for yourself what the essential elements really are.

CHAPTER 1

LET'S DO SOMETHING

Now that we have a broad idea of what brickwork is about, we can sit back and consider exactly what we want to do in our garden. We're a bit unsure of our abilities with bricks and mortar – getting things right so the neighbours won't laugh at our efforts. Worried in case we make up something and then decide, too late, that it doesn't really suit. It should be somewhere else. Not to worry. This is all about basics, and making sure the beginner *does* succeed.

MULTI-PURPOSE UNIT

We're starting with a sure-fire project. A multi-purpose garden unit, no less. And it really can't go wrong, because there are no foundations to make, no mortar work to do. We can even take our little masterpiece to bits, and shift it around as much as we want.

This is how it works.

BEGINNER'S BARBECUE

First of all, look at your garden, and consider where you would like to put, say, a handy barbecue. You'll need room to walk round it, of course. It shouldn't be in too much of a draught. You won't want leaves falling on to it from tree branches overhead. And it will make some smoke, so it can't go below any windows.

Once you decide where it *can* go, you need a suitable base. If you have settled on the existing patio, fine. Otherwise, an ordinary slab around 60 cm (2 ft) square will fit the bill beautifully. Make sure it really is flat and level, of course.

You don't need to dig a hole to make a foundation. On soil or grass, you can lay the slab on sand to make sure it has a safe, level surface. That's important.

Now you're ready for the brickwork.

Buy some suitable bricks. If in doubt, ask the man in the shop. Those with a very deep indentation on the top, known as the frog, are not the best for your needs. You are looking for ones which are as flat as possible all round.

Figure 3 shows what to do. Lay the bricks six at a time, to make a 'square circle' – in other words, a hexagon. You'll find they just fit on your slab, and if you want to use one 900 mm × 600 mm (3 ft × 2 ft), no-one is going to argue. Just have the edge of one brick touching the next, and extend this round the 'circle' to make your first course.

Next, lay six more bricks on top, to overlap the first course. Continue until you have, let's say, nine courses altogether. That should be a comfortable working height. Next, you need a piece of metal plate, from your local builders' merchant, to hold your barbecue charcoal. If you trim the corners and follow the line of the outside edges of the bricks, you will have a neat fitting. (The point is that the plate has to sit firmly on one row of bricks, but not stick out with the danger of possibly catching someone passing by.)

The next stage is to take a brick and cut it in half, with the club hammer and bolster. (Use safety goggles: it's an inexpensive investment in safety.) Mark all round. Tap along the lines you've made, firmly enough so that it breaks neatly. You are cutting it across the width. A

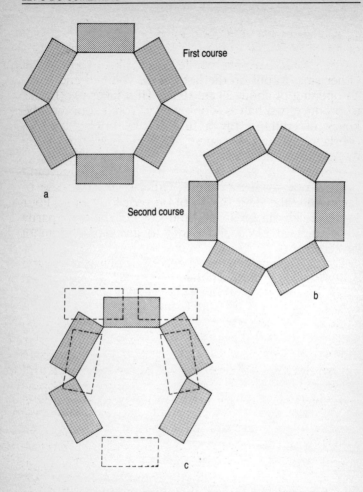

First course

Second course

a

b

c

FIG. 3 (a) *First course.* (b) *Second course.* (c) *Arrangement for top of barbecue. Note the 'open' space for draught control: four bricks to support grill.*

spare, broken brick is good for practice, to get the feel of this work.

You should have five whole bricks, plus two halves at either side, to put on the last course you laid and leave an opening of about 23 cm (9 in). (If it takes two bricks to produce two halves, don't worry. You'll soon get the knack of cutting.) Lay a further five bricks, on top, overlapping. This, of course, means you are extending the existing opening.

A grill is the next requirement. Possibly you could borrow one from the house. Otherwise, it's a case of buying one the right size to sit on your brickwork. Four more bricks can go around the sides of the grill, partly to keep it in place and partly to give some draught protection.

You will see there's now a decent-sized gap below the grill. If you're worried that it will let in too much draught, try placing a brick in the opening, on top of the metal plate, in fact.

To recap: Figure 3 shows the first course, and succeeding course. They alternate like this all the way. The metal plate is held firmly, between a complete course and one with five bricks and two halves. The grill is last, and it is held in place by four bricks. There is one spare brick available for use as a simple form of draught control if needed.

Everything is on a safe and stable base. There is room to put on the charcoal, the option of draught control, space to grill the barbecue items, and clear up afterwards. And if the spot you chose was not the best one, for whatever reason, then there's little problem in taking your barbecue to bits and putting it up somewhere else.

We could extend this building principle now to make a bigger barbecue, or we can continue with what we have learned and put the basic structure to other uses. Let's try other uses first.

The basic structure, of six bricks to a course, and each course overlapping, can easily be used for other items. This is our multi-purpose unit, after all. No point in learning a skill and not putting it to good use.

IT'S A SEAT

Try, say, six courses of bricks – that's 36 in all – possibly topped off with a 600 mm × 600 mm (2 ft × 2 ft) slab, or one slightly larger, to make a seat. Alternatively, place a piece of wood across. You will probably need a cushion for comfort, but it makes a quick and easy place to sit. And, again, there's no need at this stage to go digging holes for foundations or setting things permanently in mortar. Lots of scope to change around as required. Make two seat-bases, if you want, and join them with lengths of board and you have a bench, continuing the same building style as your barbecue.

In much the same way, taking your work up to nine courses can provide a side table – why not two, one beside the barbecue for cook to hold the ingredients, and another to eat off. Again, use a slab for the top, or a suitable piece of wood. The important point is that you make your own decisions on these aspects. It's your handiwork, after all.

It can all be done pretty quickly, with materials to hand or easily available. And if the first setting doesn't work, you can move everything to an alternative site with little fuss. You can even take it completely to bits when bad weather comes, ready to be made up again another time.

And if the lady of your life is indicating that barbecues and things are all very well, but where are those planters you promised so long ago? You know what to do. This is when you take your basic unit, and call it a planter.

IT'S A PLANTER

Make up your plant container, perhaps four courses high. Pop in a suitably sized pot, with drainage holes. Fill with decent compost, and it's ready for planting up.

A planter gives protection to the plants. It looks permanent, but can be shifted about with little trouble. It fits in with the overall style you have chosen for your first brickwork. Couldn't be better.

EARLY LESSONS

The amount of bricks? That depends on the number of courses high you are building – six to a course. Some more for a finishing top for the barbecue. The tables are about the same height, for convenience, and the chairs or seats are lower. It makes sense to get a few more bricks than you think you will need. Some may not lie properly: a few spares can always come in handy.

There was mention of taking our basic shape and modifying it to suit. That's also straightforward. Instead of using six bricks to form a hexagon shape, try eight bricks to make a larger 'circle'. You may feel this gives you a more stable structure with the bricks you have. You can adopt the same overlapping system, and you still have a draught-control system with the front bricks.

Slabs can be heavy, by the way. Get assistance in lifting and laying. If you have to do everything on your own, at least 'walk' heavy slabs by putting them edge-down onto the ground, and rocking them forward by going from one corner to the other – a 'walking' kind of motion. Alternatively, raise them carefully on to a wheelbarrow and move them that way, one at a time. Do take care not to strain muscles unused to heavy lifting.

Normal rules for family survival apply here, as in any

home-based project. When you are working with any material, look for any potential dangers – bits of brick flying about, electricity when working with power equipment, the hazards of pools and ponds with regard to small children, anything and everything – and take proper precautions.

Keep *all* animals and young children away from possible danger. Your barbecues or planters are perfectly safe and stable, but they are not suitable for use as goal posts, for practising high-wire artistes, or as mini-adventure play structures.

Materials and equipment required: a club hammer and bolster for cutting bricks; a spirit level to make sure things are horizontal or vertical; old clothes and a pair of stout gloves. A straight-edge or flat piece of wood or metal for checking that things are in a straight line, but you will find your own eye is an excellent judge of straight lines. Safety goggles are also a 'must' when cutting bricks, and they are inexpensive. You can use a piece of chalk to mark the outline for your barbecue or planter, if you wish, but moving things is very easy when they are not permanently fixed.

That completes the first practical project. The real point is that you are learning to do what *you* want – to decide where an item will go, to try it out with a dry run, and then to extend the basic size or modify the basic structure, to suit *your* requirements. Having scope to take things to bits and shift them is a bonus. It's all about trying out an idea, and getting some confidence, ready for a further step forward.

CHAPTER 2

CHEAP AND CHEERFUL

Now that we've managed to put some bricks together, and discovered we can already make interesting items for our garden, what next?

It won't have escaped notice that those hexagonal units could as easily, in most cases, have been simple squares. Let's try taking two bricks, putting one in line with another. We'll call this the first line. Lay two more, at right angles, for the second line. This is a return. Do the same again, and once more. You will notice that we have four lines of bricks. And all the sides an equal length. That's because the bricks at right angles go against the end of the corner brick. Each line makes part of *a course of bricks, two-and-a-half bricks long*. The essential point here is that each side is the same length. We now add a further course of bricks, to make an overlap all the way round. No straight lines up and down: staggered joints for strength. But still keeping the same lengths, all round.

Four courses in this manner will make an attractive planter. Put in a suitable flower pot, with drainage holes, or fill your new planter direct with suitable compost. Very little will dribble out between your evenly-laid bricks. Other square, or rectangular, items can just as easily be made up. The dimensions are entirely up to yourself: all you have to do is make sure that the opposite sides are of equal length. You should have no bricks to cut or shape, and you should have a proper overlapping joint all round.

AIMING FOR PERMANENCE

It won't have escaped anyone's notice that your barbecue, for example, was so good looking it was a shame not to make it permanent. We're now ready to make up items, using 'proper' brickwork with mortar.

With the original barbecue, all we do is make a note of the number of bricks in each course, and how they fit together. Remember the top courses, with the metal plate for the charcoal and the grill. The only brick we don't need to mortar is the one used to control the draught.

MORTAR TIME

So, on to the business of making up mortar and working with it. Figure 4 shows the equipment needed.

Mortar is the adhesive that sticks bricks together: it is moist when applied, and dries out to form a strong binding material. It used to be made with cement, sand, and hydrated lime. Nowadays, the mixture is more likely cement and sand, with what is known as a plasticizer to keep the mortar smooth and easier to work. It also helps to prevent shrinkage and cracking as the mortar dries.

Handy stuff, plasticizer. It comes in bottles, with instructions, and is really to be preferred to the washing-up liquid sometimes used!

The amount of cement and sand mixed together can differ. More cement gives a stronger mix. Adding in small stones or aggregate gives us concrete, but more of that in a later chapter. Let's take things in easy stages.

We are using ordinary bricks and we want an ordinary mortar mix. It's called a 1:6 mix because one-in-six is what it is. One part of Portland cement to six parts of

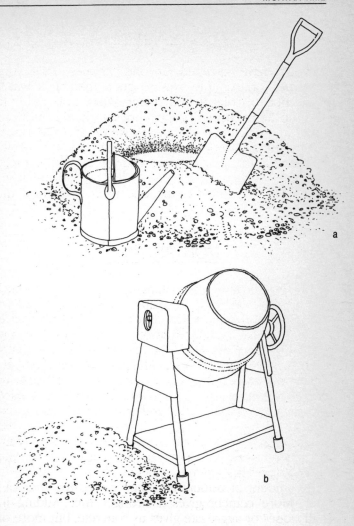

FIG. 4 (a) *To make up mortar, mix the materials thoroughly before adding water carefully – a bucket or watering can will do.* (b) *If it's extensive work, consider hiring a machine, which could be power-driven.*

clean building sand, sometimes called soft sand. We'll leave out hydrated lime and use some plasticizer instead.

In fact, with the small quantities we are using, it would not be too expensive to buy ready-made material. Ask for 1:6 mortar mix, indicate how many bricks you will be using, and your builders' merchant or garden centre will be able to oblige.

As a broad guide when it comes to larger projects, you can expect to need one bag of cement for every 400–500 bricks. And you need around 0.1 cu m (3.5 cu ft) of building sand for every 50 kg (1 cwt) bag of cement. A bag of ready-mix bricklaying mortar mix should be enough for up to 150 bricks. There are smaller amounts for smaller numbers of bricks. Ask at the builders' merchants or garden centre, to make sure you get the right amount.

Mortar is best mixed in fairly small batches. It becomes unusable in a matter of hours, and even sooner in hot weather. Ideally, choose a warm day for your brickwork project, but not too warm, and certainly avoid cold weather.

Use a clean surface, like a sheet of plywood, on which the mortar is to be mixed. Measure out the amount of sand you need, using a strong bucket as your measure. (A black polythene bucket will do.) Use another to measure out the cement, and add to the sand. With large quantities you should, ideally, use separate buckets and separate shovels for the cement, to prevent it from getting damp and going off. It's all part of the reason why ready-mixed makes sense for a first project.

However, the mixing is straightforward. You have sand and cement together. Mix them thoroughly, until you get a consistent, greyish, uniform colour. Following the instructions, add the plasticizer.

You should now have a fair pile of material, shaped like a miniature volcano. Make a small crater at the top and pour in a *little* water, from a watering can.

Keep turning over your mix, adding only small amounts of water. The aim is to end up with mortar which is fairly stiff – not soaking wet and sloppy, not simply damp powder, but firm enough to fall off the shovel cleanly. It is now ready for use.

Again, it is worthwhile trying out your new skills, using a relatively small amount of material from a ready-mix and a few spare bricks, and preferably on a piece of hardboard in an area where it can be left to dry out and used as reference. By keeping a note of the amounts you used, and the kind of weather at the time, you will soon learn what modifications are needed to meet your local situation.

MAKING SAUSAGES

Once the mortar is made, use your trowel to make a fat sausage shape, fatter in the middle than at the ends. Slide the trowel underneath, to lift your sausage, and apply it to the area marked out, ready to receive your first laid brick. Flatten the sausage to about 20 mm (¾ in) and the weight of the brick should level it to the preferred 10 mm (⅜ in) joint (see Figure 5). If not, tap the brick with the handle of the trowel. That gets it down, without damaging the brick. (A brick with an indentation, or frog, is laid face upwards.) Using a spirit level should help to ensure everything does, in fact, stay level. Lay the next brick the same way. Continue to the end of the first course.

For the return, making the right-angled corner, use the same system – make a sausage, place it on the lower brick, and let the mortar flatten to 10 mm (⅜ in) as the weight of the brick comes to bear.

There is also a 10 mm (⅜ in) joint between the bricks forming the corner. If needed, check levels and tap the

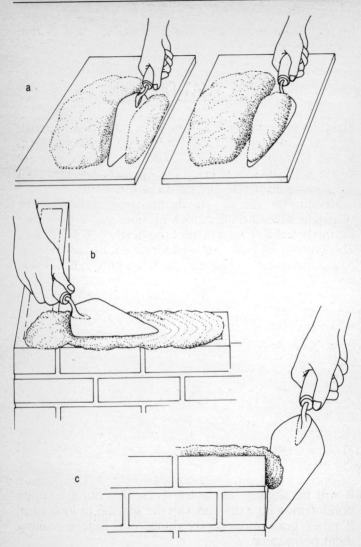

FIG. 5 (a) *Making a sausage.* (b) *Spreading it on the brickwork.* (c) *Cleaning up afterwards.*

bricks down with the trowel handle. This system continues, as required.

HIDE THAT DUSTBIN

Right, let's say we have a useful, but utilitarian, dustbin. And we want to hide it away. Not to shift it, just to keep it out of public view. We could use those concrete blocks with patterns of holes in them: very attractive, but we want to stick with brickwork at this stage.

Measure the size of your dustbin area, as a square or rectangle. Make a chalk mark for the length, and another for the breadth. Take a note of the height you need also. Then simply lay out your bricks, one course, all the way round *three* sides. (You may be hiding the dustbin, but you still have to get to it.)

This time, as you lay the bricks, allow 10 mm (⅜ in) between them. That's for the mortar we're going to be using. It's about the width of a finger, unless your gloves are too large to be used this way. Or it's the width of your piece of chalk, a diary, a bit of wood – whatever you have that fits the size as a temporary gauge.

To give an interesting appearance, and save a bit on the number of bricks used, you can make the wall an open-work or open-bond finish. (Figure 1 on page 11 shows what this looks like.) You need to turn the corner as usual, from the first course. And you also need to turn the corner for courses above. The gap between the bricks on any course is about quarter of a brick length. It will be slightly less at the ends. Try out this open bond work with a dry run. Get the spacing to look neat. It never goes amiss to try things out, before making them permanent.

You need enough space to get in to the bin, and possibly remove it. That means walls with *three* sides.

Where a wall comes to an end, and a course ends with a 'hole', fill it with a half brick. You are making space to work in, and a final size of enclosure that works out evenly, without having to cut too many bricks.

You would want some kind of top to the enclosure. Coping goes well and is laid bevelled-side up, to let the rain go off. Spread the mortar on top of the last course of bricks, with enough to take the individual length of coping you are using at a time. Keep the mortar in the joints flush with the surface but *off* the face of the bricks. A damp cloth helps here.

Continue round, using a corner piece to make things neat, and there you are. A good-looking enclosure, that is wind and waterproof. Not too high, just enough to hide the bins.

COVER THAT COMPOST HEAP

A compost heap can be hidden away in exactly the same way. Three sides, one open with some means of building up the front as the heap increases in size. The simplest way is to turn the corners, by having a single brick on either side of the opening. Then pieces of board can go behind these bricks, building up as the compost heap grows larger. The wood can be taken out, as the heap is used.

With the half bricks you would keep the cut edge inwards, and the good faces outward. Joints are made good and surfaces kept clean. A coping top keeps out the rain. Result – another straightforward addition to your garden.

Materials and equipment needed: bricks, sand, cement, mixing board, trowel, shovels, buckets. (Ready-mix.) Water. Spirit level, straight-edge. Old clothes and gloves. Club hammer, safety goggles. Board for compost heap. Chalk. Hawk.

COLD WEATHER WORKING

If the temperature is falling towards freezing, work must stop and covers put on the work. Wait until it rises to at least 2° C (35° F) before starting to lay more bricks. Cold weather slows down the hardening of the cement in mortar or concrete. Below freezing point the water in the mix turns to ice, expands, and causes havoc.

CHAPTER 3

MAKING PROGRESS

We're really on our way now. We've learned *a*) how to set up a project, measure it, make sure it fits; *b*) mix the mortar, use it properly, and finish it off; *c*) make up a unit from scratch, like the dustbin and compost enclosures. We could just about go into business on our own.

Maybe not. Laying one or two bricks doesn't really justify us in thinking we know all there is. But we're making progress, and we're gaining confidence in our ability. That certainly is worthwhile. In fact, our neighbour was so impressed with our small barbecue, he wants one for himself. Except, he wants one bigger and better. Trust the neighbour.

A BIGGER BARBECUE

So we'll make a bigger barbecue. You see it in Figure 6. Fairly straightforward. But we'll still take it slowly and carefully. It is mainly whole bricks, with a few half bricks which we can now manage comfortably.

We make sure he has the space for the one we are suggesting. We'll make sure there should be no smoke getting in the way, or trees overhead to come to any harm. There is room to move about, and it's not too far from the nearest door.

We need to start from the ground up, again. We need mortar as a base. The brickwork is built up on that. We

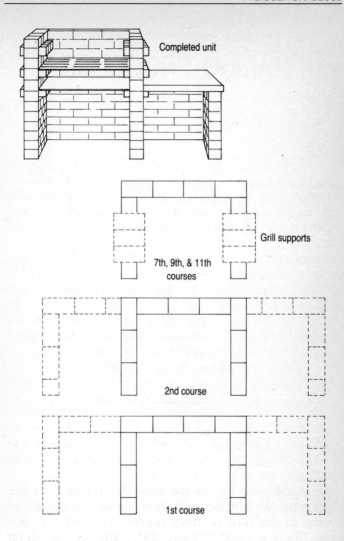

Completed unit

Grill supports

7th, 9th, & 11th courses

2nd course

1st course

FIG. 6 A larger barbecue. It can be left open, as shown, or extended on both sides and also enclosed for storage space, as shown in the plan drawings.

note that there will again be a means of putting on the charcoal safely, a metal tray or similar fuel holder. There will be a grill, to cook the food. And room for keeping food warm, above the grill – fairly sophisticated, but essentially straightforward.

Since we're making it 'bigger and better' we'll add in a fixed table top at one side. That gives storage space below. The first part of Figure 6 – 'Completed unit' – shows how it looks. And we could add a fixed top at the other side, with more storage space beneath that.

The options, in fact, would be: *a*) build only the main barbecue – an open area about 1 m (3 ft) high, and four bricks wide (four stretchers) by three deep; *b*) build the barbecue shown, with its grill area plus a worktop on the right; *c*) have *two* table tops, one either side – which is shown on the outline plan (the bird's eye view).

It's really only a matter of counting bricks now, and courses. The plan shows the barbecue area in the middle, in full outline. In *dotted outline* is the option of a table top, on either side. Take a few minutes to decide which option suits the space available, and of course have a dry run as always to get the feel of the work. Building only the barbecue unit will need a space about 90 cm × 68 cm (3 ft × 2 ft 3 in). Each table top adds about 57 cm × 68 cm (1 ft 10½ in × 2 ft 3 in), so the maximum width for the super-duper model is around 204 cm (6 ft 9 in).

As to the actual work, this is what we do.

Mark out with a piece of chalk the area you are going to use. Working from the back, the first course needs four stretchers, for the barbecue area. Add two stretchers and a header for each table top area you wish to include. Working from the barbecue area again, set two stretchers and a half brick at right angles.

Complete the table top side wall with two stretchers – i.e. each table top side wall is three bricks long, as shown in 'First course'.

That is the basic outline, but note one further point. The barbecue and table top areas are shown open at the front. If you feel happier with a more solid stucture, this is the time to remove the half bricks from the first course of the barbecue area. Put in four stretchers instead.

Similarly, if you wish your table top areas to be more solid, perhaps to be used as storage areas, simply put in two stretchers to enclose the front space in each case.

Removing those half bricks can save some cutting effort. Still, try out the work area in a dry run, to make sure you won't stub a toe against those extra stretchers. You have lots of time to try different arrangements, to find out what meets the actual needs of the situation. Keep a note of the actual option you choose, for reference when putting it together with mortar.

What you do now is add the second course, as shown in Figure 6 – 'Second course'. You will see that the barbecue and table top units simply butt together: one half brick and two stretchers, in each case, at the back. Two stretchers and a half brick make the side walls.

We have a simple bond, with staggered joints. Repeat this sequence to the sixth course.

Now for the clever bit, on the seventh course. It is shown in 'Grill Supports'. As you can surmise, these are simply bricks turned sideways, with part sticking out each side of the barbecue unit walls. Use three bricks, in the middle of the barbecue walls.

You will have the usual four stretchers at the back. Then, on the walls, a half brick, your three whole bricks turned sideways, and another half brick. You don't need any more than seven courses on your table top unit walls, by the way.

Continue the eighth course as you did the second, but only on the central barbecue unit area. That is three stretchers at the back, and three stretchers on each side wall. Still no table top additions needed yet.

For your ninth course, repeat this grill support arrangement – three bricks sideways on each barbecue unit wall. Do another course, on the central unit only, just as you did on the eighth course.

Once more, on the eleventh course, use three bricks sideways as grill supports. And once more, on the twelfth course, have three stretchers at the back, three stretchers either side.

That's about it. Except that you may have opted for one, or two table top units. If so, they will need a top – which is that old stand-by, the concrete slab, at 60 cm × 60 cm (2 ft × 2 ft). (It can be a piece of wood that size if you wish. But it's a working top, so make sure it can be kept very clean.) The sizing will allow a slight lip, for ease in handling a slab.

After the dry run, once you are satisfied with position, size, draught control, access, stability, and safety in general, it is time to make up your standard mortar. Or use ready-mix, by all means. Use a board, to keep the area clean.

Work from a 10 mm mortar base, on the patio. Keep joints to the usual 10 mm. Check verticals and horizontals with a spirit level. Clean joints of excess mortar, using a damp cloth at hand. If you are using the space below a table top for storage, a door can be hung to keep out stray animals. It is for fuel, charcoal – not inflammable charcoal lighter.

TABLE AND BENCHES

Well, now that we've had a good time with this barbecue, modestly admitting our work was not too bad for a beginner, what next?

What about a table and chair combined, something like the picnic tables the U.K. Forestry Commission provide? This is a design from Alf Kerr, who teaches all sorts of people from teenagers to old-age pensioners, how to work with bricks. That should include most of us. Figure 7(*a*) shows how it looks. Shaded bricks are *three-quarters*.

You'll see that it suits us down to the ground. Fairly straightforward, but a good design. Not too difficult and a sturdy piece of work. We'll take it in stages as usual. A patio can be the 'foundation'. Your base is set on a bed of 10 mm mortar, a bit wider than the brickwork, to make sure it is firm.

Now look at the individual components. See how it all fits together. And have a dry run to get the plan into your mind and make sure there are no unforeseen snags.

Then two beds of mortar to about 10 mm, for the two sets of brickwork. On one side, we put down a brick base, and on this we erect a small pillar to take an end of the bench. Another pillar, at the other end of the base, takes one end of the other bench. And in the middle we put up a slightly higher pillar, which is one end of our table.

Repeat on the other side, on the mortar bed we have now laid. That is – base, small pillars at the ends and larger pillar in the middle – and we have two sets of supports for our complete table and benches (Figure 7).

Our first course, then, is in fact the base as shown: one brick set sideways, and two bricks side by side at right angles to this, to a total of 12 bricks, with one more at right angles, side on. That's a total of 14 bricks.

The small pillar to take the bench is four courses of bricks, each made of two bricks side by side and the one above at right angles. That gives a good overlap or bond, with no lines running all the way through. The other end is exactly the same: four courses, each with two bricks side by side and each course at right angles to the previous one.

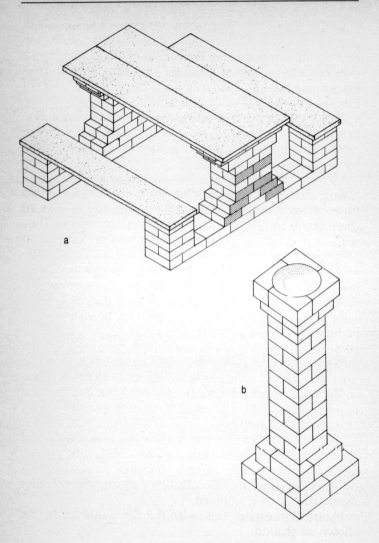

FIG. 7 (a) *Table and benches.* (b) *Birdbath, sundial.*

In the middle, for the table, are eight courses which should give enough height. On the base we made up first of all, count to the middle, and place two bricks side by side on top of this base. Put two *three-quarter* bricks side-by-side, cut faces inwards, on either side of this central pair.

That's our first bit of work, really, cutting those two bricks to three-quarter size. You could use full-size bricks, but bear with us for a moment and see what happens.

Using three-quarter bricks: Place five bricks – two three-quarters side by side, one end on, and two more three-quarters side by side – as your next course. They will 'step up' from your cut bricks beneath. Carry on with four courses now – the first one has two bricks side by side, and two bricks side by side. These are *three-quarter* bricks, now that we have learned how to cut them.

Next course has three bricks side by side but at right angles to those beneath (bonding is always needed). Back to two *three-quarter* bricks side by side, and two *three-quarter* bricks side by side, using our new skill. Another of three bricks side by side and at right angles.

The next course is four bricks, two side by side and two side by side. This gives another step-out. It's called a corbel, or crow-step.

Next course is two bricks side by side, one end on in the middle, and two bricks side by side. This gives a further step out. The last course is six bricks, two side by side, two side by side, and two more side by side. Again, this gives a step out.

Figure 7 illustrates this, with the three-quarter bricks shown as shaded.

Alternatively . . . If you really can't be bothered doing all the three-quarter brickwork, you can settle for the first course of the table support – the one immediately above the base, with six bricks in pairs, side by side – and then five courses made up of two pairs of bricks side by side.

Whatever style you have settled for on one side, you must repeat this on the other side. That gives: another base, another small pillar at one end, a similar small pillar at the other end, and the stepping-in and stepping-out support for the table in the middle.

The actual benches are most simply made of wood, one piece large enough to overlap all round slightly and give a comfortable seat. An angle iron or a bracket underneath at each side holds the wood securely to the pillars. If you really insist, bolts can be put through the wood from above, into the brickwork, countersunk, and the holes sealed with filler.

The table can have two pieces of wood, butted together or left slightly apart. Two angle irons or brackets, at either side, go into the pillars and into the wood. Bolts can also go into the top of the brickwork, on either side. Wooden battens can be fitted underneath the table top, if it is in two pieces, to make sure they stay together.

All the wood should be painted, or stained, using appropriate preservative, following the manufacturer's instructions. This has to be done *before* the wood is fixed to the pillars, of course, and it does no harm to put some preservative into boreholes for angle irons, bolts, and woodscrews.

Joints are tidied off, any split mortar is cleaned up with a damp cloth. Horizontals and verticals are checked with a spirit level.

This is a permanent, outdoor item, which will complement your permanent, outdoor barbecue and be the definite envy of everyone in the neighbourhood.

BIRD BATH, SUNDIAL

Now that we have done a fairly large project, we can look at some other, slightly smaller items. How about a bird bath or sundial, for a start?

Same procedure: decide where it is to go: have a dry run: get your material together: use a mortar base on an existing patio.

This time we have only four three-quarter bricks to deal with, and we can leave them out if we want to. The bird bath – or sundial, (Figure 7(*b*)) as taste decides – has a bed of 10 mm mortar. It has two stretchers on one side, then a header, a stretcher, and a header. That is another way of saying: first course is six bricks, arranged two side by side, one at right angles, then two at right angles side by side, the last one being at right angles again.

Next course is simply four bricks, chasing one another round the previous course – a stretcher and a header each side. This makes a step up, or in. Take nine courses of two stretchers one side, two headers the other – two bricks side by side, followed by two bricks side by side but at right angles, on to the top.

Four bricks, each being *three-quarter* bricks, chasing one another round – stretcher one side, header the other – like the second course you made, give you a stepping-out effect. A last course of four bricks – stretcher and header each side – chasing one another round and exactly like the second course, will give another step out.

If you prefer not to cut bricks, you simply leave out the second-top course or make it a repeat of the nine previous ones.

The bird bath you get from a garden centre or pet shop. Fix it in, using the open space in the brickwork to take the bowl.

If you prefer a sundial, that should be large enough to be set on the actual bricks. Strictly speaking, you should go for a sundial 'set' to your particular longitude, and decide on daylight time, standard time, mean time, summer time, or whatever. (Most people use a wrist-watch anyway.)

To keep things tidy, make sure each course is properly finished, with a secure joint and no mortar spilled. If it is, clean it up with a damp cloth. Your horizontals and verticals are checked with a spirit level.

With any project, if rain is expected cover the work with a sack, a large cloth, a polythene bag or whatever is handy. Leave brickwork to set, before putting any kind of pressure on it.

Materials and equipment required: bricks, sand, cement, mixing board, trowel, spirit level, straight-edge. Club hammer, bolster, safety goggles. Buckets, shovels, water. Timber, saw, preservative, screwnails, screw-driver, bolts and nuts, spanner. Old clothes, gloves. Damp cloth.

CHAPTER 4

A SURE FOUNDATION

Now that we have built up some confidence, we can turn our attention to more adventurous projects, that need foundations. In this way, we're doing three things – coming to terms with foundations, and with concrete; looking at walls; and doing an easy project to keep our confidence in good order.

In fact, we've been doing a bit of foundation work as we've gone along. Making sure we know what we are doing at each stage, getting accustomed to handling bricks, cutting them, and placing them. Checking our measurements, getting things level, and straight. Making items we want, for our own gardens. Or for our friends. That's what we're about.

With walls, it is worth remembering that they are not particularly stable when free standing, unless they are on good foundations. Make these good and deep. Check with neighbours who may know about local walls that were blown down in a gale. Ask how deep the founds went, or didn't.

Short walls are less prone to damage. And open-bond walls are like hedges: they break the force of the wind by letting a lot of it through.

Look back at Figure 1 (p. 11). It reminds us that loads should be spread widely. That is what a foundation is for. Compare someone wearing high heels with weight concentrated on one small area, to someone wearing snow-shoes that let weight spread over a wider than usual area.

CONCRETE PROGRESS

The next working stage is learning about concrete. It's like mortar, but a good deal stronger. And our projects can include walls, in a variety of shapes and sizes. The previous projects were about as large as could be made, without using a proper foundation.

Let's get this concrete business sorted out. At its simplest, a general purpose mix would be of the order of 1:2:4. That means one measure (e.g. a bucket) of cement, two of sharp sand, and four of a coarse aggregate. We'll use the 1:6 mix for mortar and this 1:2:4 for concrete throughout.

Try to use a separate shovel and bucket for the cement, to keep it dry and prevent spoiling.

If you have a large, heavy-duty polythene bucket it will hold about 14 l (3 gal) of water, or about 20 kg (44 lb) of cement. That's heavy.

Consult your local builders' merchant for advice, on amounts for a given piece of work. They are dealing in these materials daily, and can help the amateur enormously.

This is as good as time as any for some DIY. A 2.44 m × 1.22 m (8 ft × 4 ft) ply board cut in half gives two pieces 1.22 m × 1.22 m (4 ft × 4 ft). One makes a mixing board. The other, cut diagonally, gives two right-angle triangles, or one could be used to make a hawk.

Alternatively, three pieces of wood in the proportions of three, to four, to five, give a right-angle triangle as we learned, and probably forgot, at school.

The other item to make is a gauge rod, a piece of wood with shallow saw cuts every 75 mm (3 in) which mark the courses of a wall.

Going back to our concrete, whatever amount you need, it has to be mixed properly. There are three basic options: mixing by hand, mixing by machine, or having it delivered in bulk.

Doing it yourself, work carefully, and methodically. You need a mixing platform, like your piece of hardboard. Two shovels and two buckets preferably. A watering can, using water from the tap, not stagnant water from a butt or pond. Cement and sharp sand. Coarse aggregates, which are small stones from a builders'.

Measure the sand and aggregates as required. Make a crater on top of the pile, and tip in the cement. Mix thoroughly, turning it over until it looks uniformly one colour throughout. Make another crater and gradually pour in water, using no more than half the expected amount.

Mix and turn until this amount is all used, before adding any more. Gradually add some, to provide a smooth, moist mix, not too dry and crumbly and not too sloppy. Slap the top of the pile with your shovel. If water runs out, it is too wet. Add a small amount of cement and aggregates, in the right proportions, and mix again. Test again.

In practice, it means mixing the materials at least twice dry, and three times wet.

This is admittedly laborious and can cause problems of consistency even for experienced workers. Hiring a cement mixer helps with the work – it should come with instructions, and a reminder to wash it out after use.

The easy way, for large areas at least, is to order up ready-mixed cement from a tanker. Be sure that you have space to take it when the vehicle arrives, discharging to a large polythene sheet, and lots of helpers to get the material to the right place in time. Wheelbarrows help enormously but have to be cleaned up afterwards also.

As with everything else, take it carefully. Try a small area of work first. Get a bit of experience before branching off into large-scale projects. Get advice from your builders' merchant, and from any neighbours who have done concreting already.

BASIC WALLS

A typical project would be to lay a foundation for a free-standing brick wall. The U.K. Brick Development Association, incidentally, recommends leaving out flexible damp proof courses at ground level: the mortar 'slides' about.

Mark out the area. Use softwood pegs with a cross-piece at each end. Hammer in nails into each cross-piece to mark the width of the trench to be dug out. Stretch a line between the two cross-pieces. Mark the area with a sprinkling of sand under the two lines. Dig out the trench within the outlined area to the required depth. See Figure 8(*a*).

The top of the foundation would be about 300 mm (12 in) below ground level, to protect it against possible ground movement caused by weather conditions.

Drive in other pegs, to protrude by the depth of concrete needed. Use a spirit level on straight-edged wood to check levels are consistent. Pour in the concrete. Get rid of any air bubbles by 'slicing' at the concrete with a shovel.

Compact the concrete, using a straight-edged piece of wood, to make sure the surface is level with the pegs you put in. Remove pegs and fill these holes with concrete. Figure 8(*a*) shows the idea.

On ordinary soil, for a wall half a brick thick, you would have 150 mm (6 in) of concrete. The foundation would be about 300 mm (12 in) wide and about 150 mm (6 in) longer at either end than the actual wall. In other words, have good strong foundations, deep enough and

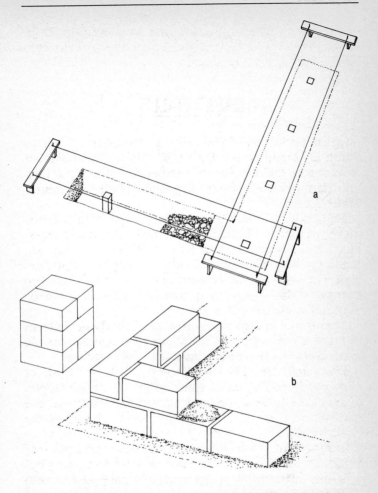

FIG. 8 (a) *Strip foundations need a trench, filled with hard-core, 'blinded' with sand to fill any gaps, then concrete laid to the level of the guide pegs.* (b) *When laying the bricks, lay half a dozen along each arm of a wall, checking with a spirit level. Do the same at the other corner, stretch a line across and fill in the central area.*

spread out to take the load, for a wall no more than 1.2 m (4 ft) high.

As a guide, this half-brick wall would need about 60 bricks for 1 sq m or 54 for 1 sq yd. A half-brick wall in open bond would require fewer bricks: about 50 to 1 sq m or 40 to 1 sq yd.

So far, we have simply made up our walls as we went along. The professional way is to do each corner, checking levels (Figure 8(*b*)). Then put a line right across, to give the level of the course and fill in the middle portion – like doing a giant jigsaw puzzle.

CURVED WALLS

You can also make curved walls, of course – sometimes called serpentine, for obvious reasons. What you do is draw out, say, an elliptical shape using sand to show the outline. You can use two pegs, loop a length of twine round, place a stick against the twine and mark out your shape that way. Alter the size of the loop until you get a shape you like. There's pragmatism for you.

A short, curved half-brick wall could be made up to give variety. Used on a patio, it would not need any concrete founds. The mortar arrangements already mentioned would suffice.

Most walls, however, are straight and one brick wide. They require foundations about 450 mm (18 in) wide and the same deep. The concrete is 150–230 mm (6–9 in) on top of that. That takes a wall up to about 1.2 m (4 ft) high.

Lots of walls are built with smaller amounts of found, and stay up. Still, it's better to be safe than sorry.

Various bonds are shown in Figure 9, and the arrangements to turn corners. As usual, it is easier to show than to explain. This also shows how a pier is made, in the middle of a long wall, and at each end for strength and stability. With piers, you extend the foundations outwards an appropriate distance. ∴

Note that the middle pier on a half-brick wall is made using two header bricks, in place of one stretcher, at about 1.8 m (6 ft) intervals, or closer if felt appropriate.

The second course has two *three-quarter* stretchers with a *half-brick* in between – that makes up the total of two bricks to give the running bond.

The end pier on a half-brick wall is simply a brick against the end stretcher, with a *half-brick* butted into the corner. The second course ends with a stretcher and another stretcher behind it.

RETAINING WALLS

A retaining wall has to be strong. It's holding up an entire bank of earth, after all. Half-brick walls are not suitable.

Mark out the area. Make the trench, to leave the top of the concrete about 300 mm (12 in) below ground level. Remember some weep holes for the bricks, to let water drain away. And move the earth out of the way first. Give yourself room to move.

For piers on a full-brick wall, a typical bonding system would be to make the bottom four or six courses one and a half bricks thick. The first course is stretcher and header alternately. Behind that, it is header and stretcher – making the one and a half thickness – with a *half brick* in the space in the middle. The second course is the same pattern, but reversed, to give a bond.

The full-brick courses have a header at the end, and two stretchers edge to edge alternately. Over this are two stretchers edge to edge, and a header, alternately.

There are many bonds or patterns available for full-

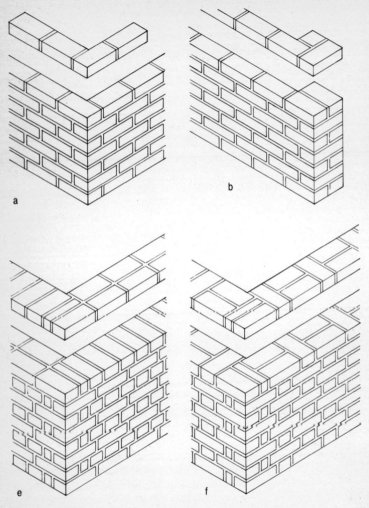

FIG. 9 *Keeping up with the bonds. The selection includes* (a) *stretcher bond corner;* (b) *end pier;* (c) *mid pier;* (d) *stopped end;* (e) *English bond corner (note the slim queen closer to stagger joints;* (f) *Flemish bond corner (same queen closer*

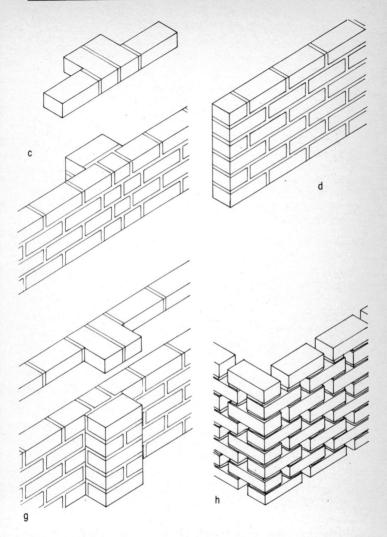

usage); (g) stretcher bond mid pier (with two three-quarter bricks and one half-brick on the lower course); (h) some attractive open bond.

brick working. One to consider is English garden wall bond. There are three courses of stretchers, two bricks edge to edge to give the full width required, and then one course of headers. On the header courses, a thin piece of brick is used, to stagger the joints. This is made by cutting a brick in half, lengthwise, and is known as a *queen closer*.

The closers are used between the last and second last headers. Turn the corner by using the last stretcher as the first header, put in the *queen closer* you have found out about, and continue the bond as before.

The whole idea of brickwork probably sounds terribly confusing by now, and tiring. So here are some timely reminders:

There is no need to rush at things. Get some idea of how long it will take – that's why a dry run is so helpful. Check out the price. Don't overstretch yourself either financially or physically.

If you are not accustomed to this kind of work, take it easy. You have all the time there is. It's supposed to be for pleasure, after all. And remember to clean up and change your shoes before you go indoors.

WALLS AS CONTAINERS

If all this business of deep foundations sounds just a bit too much, and you've started feeling unsure about your abilities, let's try an easy project to get the confidence back. Look at Figure 10. It couldn't be simpler.

It suggests four boxes. And an open space in the middle. The four boxes can give you four planters, and a pool in the middle. Or cover the boxes with a square of wood each, and you now have four seats, and a pool – or a planter, if you prefer. Or any permutation you want. On an existing patio, you don't even need to make

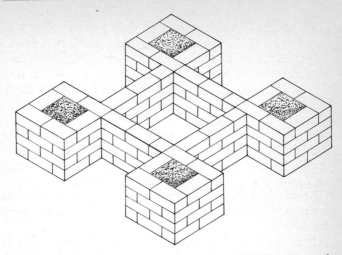

FIG. 10 They are just little boxes put together. But they can make planters, pools, seats – anything you like, really.

concrete foundations. Mortar will do. All you really do is make four square boxes – planters or seats, as you decide – and join them with four small walls.

This is a good project to meet the needs of elderly or handicapped people, who cannot always get about as much as they would like but still want to be out in the garden.

Take the basic format, which suggests four courses of brickwork. Make the planters and walls higher if you wish. Extend the joining walls, to give access to a wheelchair, perhaps. Use only two planters. Use only two walls. Leave a space in between. Your ideas are as good as anyone else's. These are building blocks, to be modified as you require – after a dry run, of course. Always try out your ideas before committing yourself to a final decision.

To recap, Figure 10 shows a structure which is the

size of six-and-a-half bricks square. That lets you draw an outline, with chalk, on your patio. Again, check everything is square before starting. Decide what sizes you are going to use.

Lay a bed of mortar about 15 mm (1½ in) deep. Make one square box on this, checking horizontal and vertical surfaces with a spirit level. Make sure the joints are clean and tidy. Leave no mortar spilled on the patio or the brickwork you are producing. The square is, as already indicated and shown in the drawing, two bricks one way and one-and-two-half bricks the other – two stretchers, then a header with a stretcher and a header.

Your mortar bed will have to extend right across, to take in the joining wall if you are using one, and then to the next square box. We are not looking to make any fancy joins between squares and walls. They simply go together as required.

The walls, as the drawing shows, are two-and-a-half bricks for one course, then half a brick and two bricks, to give an overlap or bond – two stretchers and a header. Repeat this to four courses as shown.

Repeat, with a 15 mm (½ in) bed of mortar for each box, and each wall. Keep straight vertically and horizontally. Keep the joins smooth. Keep the mortar off the brick faces and off the patio, using a damp cloth as necessary.

The drawing suggests the boxes should be left open. This lets you make them into planters – by adding compost and, not forgetting in this case, small weep-holes in the bottom course to allow excess moisture, or rain, to drain out.

Or you make them into seats by putting a piece of wood over the top course, at whatever height you did, in fact, decide was suitable. Use preservative on the wood and retain the wood with bolts into the brickwork, the bolts being countersunk and the holes filled with sealer.

The central area is a planter if you wish, again using suitable compost and remembering weep-holes in the bottom course to let rain out. It becomes a pool by putting in a suitable size of rigid liner, seated on 50–75 mm (2–3 in) of sand, and the surrounding space back-filled with soil to keep it firmly placed.

Materials and equipment: bricks, sand, cement, aggregates, mixing board, buckets and shovels, water. Spirit level, straight-edge. Club hammer, bolster, safety goggles. Timber, saw, pegs, nails, preservative. Old clothes, gloves.

CHAPTER 5

STEPPING UP

Now we're making progress. In fact, we're thinking of what else needs doing in the garden. We're taking steps to improve the layout, make easier access, get from one place to another.

Let's start with a look at what we might call straight steps, simply going from one level to another. Nothing fancy. And nothing beyond our capabilities. We know the essentials, after all.

Consider what it is we want to do, and why. Are steps really necessary or just a whim? Will they make things easier – to get to the drying green area, to the vegetables, or whatever? Would the family much prefer a safe walk down steps rather than slither down a grassy slope? Then we're in business.

We know where the steps should go, and we know what is needed. First, check the site and decide the dimensions. Consider what slope there is – how do we get over the hurdle of different levels? How many steps will there be, what width, and so on.

We'll do a few examples again, in different situations.

VARIETIES OF STEPS

Basically, there are the two kinds of steps in a garden – those built into an existing slope and those that are free-standing, joining two different levels. For comfort and safety, any set of steps should be evenly spaced.

Preferably, they should be at least 610 mm (2 ft) wide. This is a minimum. Two's company and that needs at least 1.4 m (4 ft 6 in) of width. In fact, if you do a check on any stately homes and gardens you visit, you'll probably agree that wide, sweeping steps are much to be preferred to narrow ones – where it is possible.

The terms used are: treads (the parts you tread, or walk on) and the risers (the upright parts). Walking up steps is easier with long treads and relatively low risers. And since an average-size man's foot is about 1 ft long – that's how it got the name – you really don't want a tread any shorter than 300 mm (12 in).

Slabs are popular as treads, and there is no reason to ignore this: bricks are excellent for combining with other materials. If you want a slab top, that's fine.

That could give risers, for example, of 100 mm (4 in) from one course of bricks laid flat, plus a 25 mm (1 in) slab; 113 mm (4.5 in) from one course of bricks on edge, or a course laid flat plus a 38 mm (1½ in) slab; 125 mm (5 in) from one course laid flat and a 50 mm (2 in) slab on top; 150 mm (6 in) from two courses laid flat; 165 mm (6½ in) from one course on edge and a 50 mm (2 in) slab; or even 180 mm (7 in) from two courses laid flat and a 25 mm (1 in) slab.

Brick is a very 'friendly' material. It gives great flexibility in working out solutions to everyday problems.

DOING THE SUMS

You will need to decide on the number of treads and risers for any given flight of steps. Select your two levels, put in pegs and check the (vertical) difference in height. Check also the length of ground for free-standing steps or the slope for built-in ones.

A gentle slope 1.8 m (6 ft) long with a 610 mm (2 ft) difference in height, and a low riser of 100 mm (4 in) would mean 610 mm divided by 100 mm = 6 steps. (24 in divided by 4 in is also 6 steps.) The tread would be 300 mm (12 in). Making the tread 460 mm (18 in) would give 4 steps: 1.8 m (6 ft) divided by 460 mm (18 in) = 4.

One more example: free-standing steps over a distance of 1.5 m (5 ft) and a height difference of 0.9 m (3 ft). Using 300 mm (12 in) treads, there would be 5 steps: 1.5 m (5 ft) divided by 310 mm (1 ft) = 5. This would allow 180 mm (7 in) risers.

Don't worry too much about exact sums. There are always minor inaccuracies to be dealt with in this kind of work, as you go along. A dry run is never going to go amiss.

You put in pegs to fix two parallel lines, as far apart as the step width, and from top to bottom of the slope. Measure the length. Measure the height difference. Assistance can be sought. If you have to do it solo, measure in convenient stages with a spirit level on a flat piece of wood or similar straight-edge.

Decide your number of steps. Mark the front edge of each step, evenly spaced, and at right angles to the lines you set first. Your builder's square comes in here – it's 3:4:5 as you remember, or your piece of ply. Now shape the ground for each step, with a spade, beginning at the foot to work from a flat area.

PATHWAY WITH STEPS

A short pathway with steps works like this.

Use concrete for the foundation, let it set, and lay a path of bricks in a chosen pattern. Form a riser, on the back of the path, continue with bricks as a tread in a different pattern, allowing a slight overlap at the front edge, a riser on the tread and so on, on to the top where the steps join another short path. Mortar is used to set the bricks. Figure 11(*a*) shows what happens.

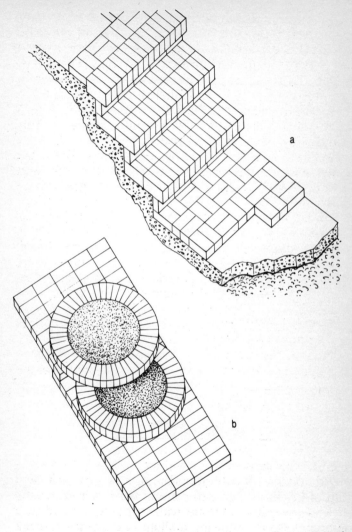

FIG. 11 (a) *With steps, from a pathway, concrete is usually to be preferred to hard-packed earth.* (b) *Circular steps are a possibility provided there is enough space.*

As an alternative, and incorporating slabs, the footing strip could have a trench 125 mm (5 in) deep for the first riser. That would be 125 mm (5 in) wide for a single line of bricks, laid flat.

Use the 1:2:4 concrete mix discussed in Chapter 4. Mortar is the 1:6 mix of Chapter 2.

Now wait overnight, before building up the first riser on this strip. Let your 10 mm (⅜ in) mortar base dry for about two hours before ramming down hard-core for the first tread behind the riser. Do not disturb the brickwork and mortar. Lay your bricks or slab tread, allowing a *slight* downward slope for drainage. The slab should project about 25 mm (1 in) over the riser.

Build the next riser on the back edge of this first tread, making sure the riser is vertical. Continue to the top, which should be level with the ground. Fill between brick or slab treads with mortar or sharp sand. Let mortar set for about a day before allowing any use of the steps. Check as you go with a spirit level, horizontally and vertically.

To recap: the first riser is on a solid footing strip, a tread is laid on that with a firm fill underneath. Each succeeding riser goes on the back of the previous tread, and there is a slight drainage slope.

FREE-STANDING STEPS

Free-standing steps are similar, except that they are supported on side walls, the area between filled with hard-core as a base. The side walls are on a concrete footing strip, using normal 1:2:4 concrete mix. This copes with up to five steps. Above that, a concrete sub-base for the whole structure is recommended practice.

Decide where the steps are to go. Measure the space available, and determine the height difference as before. Decide the number of steps, and dimensions of risers and treads. A 125 mm (5 in) layer of concrete is used.

Again, wait about a day for the concrete to harden before making the supporting walls.

These are made up course by course. They form an open box, in effect, filled in with hard-core. Treads rest on these walls and the hard-core bed. Use mortar to the normal 1:6 mix. Slabs would project about 25 mm (1 in) and there should be a *slight* downward slope for drainage.

Wait at least two hours for a brick mortar to set before filling in the areas between walls and risers with hard-core. There is no rush in this kind of work. Be careful not to disturb newly laid bricks or fresh mortar. Fill any gaps with mortar, including the gap under any slabs used. Clean up brick faces as you go along, with a damp cloth.

OTHER KINDS OF STEPS

If you are putting steps alongside an existing wall, that will mean toothing it in – cutting out bricks to anchor it in. A brick from each course on the steps has to go into the existing wall – half on the course, half into the wall – by making an appropriate opening in this wall. It can be a daunting thought. Check what you have in mind. This is another case where a dry run pays dividends.

Curved steps can be made, using timber as a former for the edging. Saw cuts at 125 mm (5 in) intervals should cater for most curves required. Circular steps are attractive. Their only drawback is that they require a fair bit of space, and a fair number of bricks. However, construction is as for any other form of steps. A firm foundation, risers as required, and treads on the risers. See Figure 11(*b*).

Materials and equipment: spade, pegs, string, hammer and nails, timber, saw. Spirit level, set square, trowel, mixing board, buckets and shovels. Cement, sand and aggregate. Old clothes, gloves. Sacking or polythene for cover as required.

CHAPTER 6

STEPPING OUT

Paths and patios are popular features of any garden. There has to be some means, after all, of getting about reasonably dry-shod, and of sitting out in the sun with a long, long cooling drink after a hard day's work.

We will be looking at some of the many variations available to the amateur, and concentrating on brick-work. These are by no means the only possibilities of course, and there is indeed a companion volume, called *Paths, Patios and Paving*, which goes into greater detail.

THE REQUIREMENTS

What we want are the two basic requirements – getting about from one place to another, and sitting out in comfort on a paved area. We can call in the contractors, or we can do it ourselves. Can we manage on our own? This is what is involved.

Look at the garden. Decide what you want, and where. Some place for drying clothes, a vegetable patch, sweeping lawns, a greenhouse, a garden shed, a paddling pool or sand pit for the kids ... the list can be endless. So you mentally divide the whole area into its constituent parts, to meet your family needs, and go ahead from there. Be guided by your own usage. If you take a particular line from A to B, then that is the line of your path, ready decided.

What you will be doing is deciding the line of the path, making foundations for it, putting in retaining edging, and filling in the spaces in the middle. Using brickwork, you have a wide choice of patterns. Some are shown in Figure 12.

Be fairly generous with space, make paths at least 1.4 m (4 ft 6 in) wide if you can, so that two can walk together. A very narrow path, between bushes, can make for awkward passage. Mostly, paths will not need any camber or slope, but if there is any slope it has to allow rain or surface water to run off to the sides.

PATIOS

Patios, in a way, are paths on a large scale. The point is that patios often link house and garden. They are an extension of the garden, almost into the house – sometimes literally so. And they are an extension of the house to the outside.

To an extent, you are limited in where a patio can go and usually it will be at the back, or side, of the house because that is where a doorway has already been provided. At this stage, we are not intending making new doors or adding on sunrooms. We are simply looking at the existing property, and trying to improve it to meet our own needs.

Since a patio is a hard, flat surface, it has to be borne in mind that this surface must always be *below* the existing damp proof course and air bricks in the house. You can't put in a patio that directs rain water against the wall or even into the foundations of the house itself.

A patio should also slope gently away from the house to keep rain water at bay. It forms a kind of dry moat around your property.

We will stick to simple patterns – it saves on the hard work involved – but it is important to make sure paths

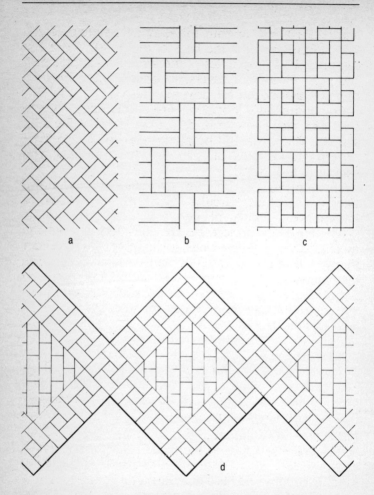

FIG. 12 A great variety of patterns can be made with brickwork. (a) Herringbone, which can be laid straight or zig-zag; (b) cane-weave; (c) squared design with a cut block filling the gap in the centre; (d) a splendid old pattern, dating from 1875, and still in use in an English garden.

and patios blend in with the existing building. If you have a facing brick at the back of the house, see if you can possibly find supplies of the same bricks for a path and patio. Paviors, or pavers, are excellent for this kind of work and indeed for driveways also.

Colour-mixing is not necessary at this stage: stick to one brick face and one brick colour. It makes life a lot simpler. There will still be plenty of scope for pleasant patterns. Patios, after all, can cover a large area. You want it to look good.

The patterns can be formal, straight up and down lines, or include circular elements – perhaps to incorporate a circular planter.

As with every project we are considering, even the most apparently simple ones, it is important to consider the overall situation carefully and in some depth. See the finished work in your mind's eye. Draft it out on paper. Discuss it with your family. Get their approval and if possible get their practical support.

Then it is down to work.

PATHS

Paths on firm, well-rolled ground can sometimes suffice, but digging down to allow for a 100 mm (4 in) layer of hard-core, well rammed down, makes for a firmer result. The edging has to be fixed first, same base, on a bed of 1:2:4 concrete. In the middle area goes a layer of sand, over rammed hard-core, around 50 mm (2 in) or so to take the bricks for the pathway.

Standard lengths of edging are available, for contrast with the bricks or paviors, and are similarly set on concrete over a hard-core base.

A less expensive alternative for a path would be wood, with preservative if it is to remain permanently, or simply removed once the path itself has been laid and set firm. Permanent wood edging would ideally be bought as pre-treated with vacuum-pressure preservative.

Wood comes into its own when making a curved path, held in place with pegs behind the timber. Cuts at 125 mm (5 in) intervals should allow the wood to take up most curves without breaking. Check heights and any slope, as usual.

Try to get hard-wearing bricks: specify that is what you need, for outdoor use. You are looking for about 40 for a square metre or 36 a square yard, laid flat. On edge that becomes more like 50 and 45 respectively.

Mark out your area with pegs and lines. The bricks are laid on a 50 mm (2 in) bed of sand. The sand is screeded, made flat using a stout board. It may need two people to use it properly. Check levels regularly, tapping down any high bricks with the end of a trowel or piece of wood. Fill in the surface gaps with sand or a dry mixture of sand and cement. This can be brushed in, and then watered in carefully. Avoid splashing mortar on to the face of the bricks. It has to be cleaned off, with a damp cloth, and takes a lot of time on a large area.

PAVIORS

Paviors are an alternative, more expensive but harder wearing and generally a better looking finish. They are not standard brick size: more like 200 mm × 100 mm × 65 mm which takes 50 to a square metre or 42 to a square yard. Paviors of 215 mm × 215 mm dimension would need 20 to a square metre and 18 to a square yard.

They take a similar sub-base of rammed hard-core to 100 mm (4 in) or so, and a 65 mm (2½ in) bed of sand compacted to 50 mm (2 in) once the blocks are laid.

On grass, paths and patios are often laid just below surface level. This allows easier lawn-mowing.

In any case, the benefit of working with a sand bed for the main area of path or patio is that you do get a dry run to check progress.

You can see how the patterns fit, what spaces are left, and how many bricks or paviors are in fact being used. A slight camber, from the middle, takes care of surface water.

Any spaces in a pattern are filled in, as appropriate, with half bricks, gravel, aggregate, cobble stones, whin chips – whatever suits your style.

Bricks can be cut to shape, carefully, using a club hammer and chisel but it is not easy to get accurate shaping. They can also be cut with a hydraulic press or a stone-cutting saw. These are not normal items in the amateur's garden shed, but they can sometimes be hired. If a neighbour has a similar project, consider sharing the cost and saving time against a given expenditure.

The area involved in a patio is normally much larger than for a path. You have to be more particular here, and not depend solely on visual judgement.

PEG IT OUT

Mark out the area with pegs. Use a builder's square (3:4:5 dimensions for pieces of timber or your ply triangle) as necessary. Remove ground material to allow for a hard-core base, well compacted. Provide stable edging, on hard-core and concrete. Fill the central area with a layer of screeded sand, over the hard-core. Lay the bricks or paviors in the desired pattern on your flat bed of sand.

Check for a fall, keeping it constant. Remember a slight camber to remove surface water. Work in reasonable-sized areas, around 1.5 m (5 ft) at a time each way. Use more pegs as necessary to check distances and levels.

Pause and check that everything is working out right. Again, take your time on this kind of project, and get it right.

Working to a sloping surface, you will have to work out a slope, or fall, for the path or patio. Two pegs, at a suitable interval, and a cross piece for a spirit level, show when the surface is flat and level.

Putting one peg farther in gives a fall or slope. Cut a small piece of wood, placed on the lower peg, to take up the level again. When the small piece of wood, the shim, is in place the spirit level should show the bubble to be level. Take away spirit level and shim, and the two pegs give the required slope (Figure 13).

Actual dimensions are not critical. The requirement is to be consistent along the length of ground involved. For a patio, hiring a plate vibrator may be worthwhile. It is a bit hard on paths, but helps to settle a large patio area well.

Use two shovels and two buckets if possible, keeping one of each for the cement, to keep it dry as long as possible. A garden rake can spread the concrete, being cleaned as you go along. A straight-edge of wood tamps down the concrete, to expel any air before it sets. (Using a concave piece of wood will give you an automatic camber.) A steel float smooths off the concrete surface.

Materials and equipment: mixing board, trowel, sand, cement, aggregates, spirit level, builder's square, pegs, string. Wood, hammer, nails. Wheelbarrow. Cement mixer (hired). Old clothes, gloves. Damp rag.

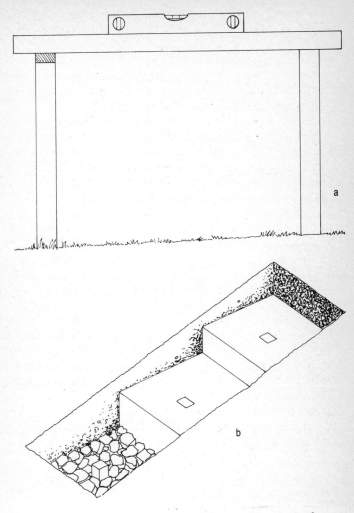

FIG. 13 (a) *For a required slope, use a shim, a thin piece of wood of the correct thickness.* (b) *For foundations on a slope, a stepped trench is needed. Pegs are used to give the different levels.*

CHAPTER 7

DRIVE ON

Essentially, this means looking at existing driveways – to modify them or repair any damage that has taken place over the years – or considering putting down a new one. These can be major projects and are not to be undertaken lightly.

If, for example, a driveway is constantly submerged by weeds, there are gaps here and there with missing bricks, and many are chipped or loose, there is a clear possibility that the foundation work simply was not properly done. Or again, there could have been some work in the past that involved digging up a section of the driveway – looking for an underground pipe, for example – and the repairs have not been completed satisfactorily.

The latter case is the simplest to solve – have the workmen put things right, to your satisfaction. That should really have been part of the agreement made before the work began. If, however, you are looking at the ravages of time, and a splendid annual crop of hard-to-budge weeds, is it perhaps time for a complete replacement?

Take up some of the driveway – where the weeds are thickest, naturally – and see what kind of base there is. It should be well-packed aggregate, with a further base on top of that of sand or similar inert material on which the brickwork has been laid. Ideally, there would be something like heavy-gauge polythene below the sand. That is what keeps the weeds at bay.

ASSESSMENT

If not, you will have to decide both the time and probable cost involved in taking everything up, and putting it right. Be realistic in your assessment: it is your time and money that is involved. It may well be that you will require completely new bricks, plus reasonably thick polythene, plus a sand and mortar mix for the finished work.

You also have to retain an access, at least to the house, while the work is in progress. And you will need some place to park the car. Will a neighbour oblige: will a neighbour object? All these things have to be considered beforehand. You can't start and then stop halfway. How long did it take to do other brickwork projects? How long is it before the summer holidays come round? Have you any important visitors due? – and so on.

IMPROVING AN OLD DRIVE

Assuming you decide on complete renovation, then have a dry run first – mentally removing all the existing items, getting down to the base, killing off growth with suitable weed-killer, putting in the covering of polythene, laying 50 mm (2 in) of level sand, and placing the new, unbroken bricks. Take it step by step, put it down on paper. Have a very clear picture in your mind of what you will be doing.

If anyone else in the neighbourhood has the same idea, go and see how he is getting on. Lend a hand, even. Have a look around for contractors putting up a drive-in fast-food place, or doing up a pedestrian precinct. See what time is involved with the professionals, and multiply it by three.

What you end up with will be a worthwhile project

for your own drive. There are a number of patterns that you can use. Those for paths, shown in Chapter 6, will do fine. The simpler the better, with few cut bricks involved. They all operate on having a boundary, edging, and a pattern to fill in.

Ordinary bricks can be used – making sure you specify hard-wearing ones – but it is often worthwhile specifying paviors. These slightly squarer bricks are much harder wearing. This is what you see on filling station driveways, in precincts, and other outdoor areas with lots of traffic. They usually have no indentations on which surface water can collect. They are also more expensive. You get what you pay for in this world.

PATTERN POSSIBILITIES

Figure 12 (p. 64) shows a selection of pattern possibilities: herringbone, cane weave, a 'square' design and an old pattern dating from 1875. With the herringbone pattern you need cut bricks to fill in the small shapes left at the sides, and mortar or gravel to fill in the smallest parts that are missing.

A NEW DRIVEWAY

For a completely new driveway, the basics are as indicated already. But be assured, this is a major project, and not something to be entered into lightly. Decide the line of the drive. See whether it will take the width of the car. If necessary run the car on to the 'drive' to make sure. Do the car doors open; can you see where you are going in reverse; will snow fall off the roof in winter and cover the car, or whatever? A dry run here is advisable.

Once you have decided the line, you have to dig it out. Grass is relatively soft, but a new house, for example, might have fairly compacted so-called topsoil to deal with. Hiring equipment may well be sensible.

The strength of the foundations and sub-base determines the ability of the drive surface to support heavy loads. It has to be firm and stable. It also needs to be at least 3 m (10 ft) wide, in order to let car doors open, or let people walk past the car when it is parked.

There has to be a slight camber, to let rain water drain from the surface. It also has to slope away from the house. If you are making a new driveway as an entrance to your property, get in touch with the local authority first. Remember to ask them about putting in a low kerb to give you easier access over the pavement as well.

DESIGN FIRST

A driveway is like making a very large-size path, so take it in easy stages. A design on paper first. Size things up. Estimate materials needed. And time. And money. Then start.

Put in pegs and line to mark the edges of the driveway, allowing for any permanent edging to go in. Check with a measure that widths are constant along the driveway. Use a 3:4:5 builder's square for right-angled corners. Your piece of ply is probably too small for this work. It helps to mark the pegs, to show the depths of different layers.

USING POLYTHENE

Without concrete, the base has to be filled with aggregate and packed down firmly. Use smaller pieces to save leaving any voids or empty spaces. A measure of sand can cover this, to leave a smooth surface. Then you

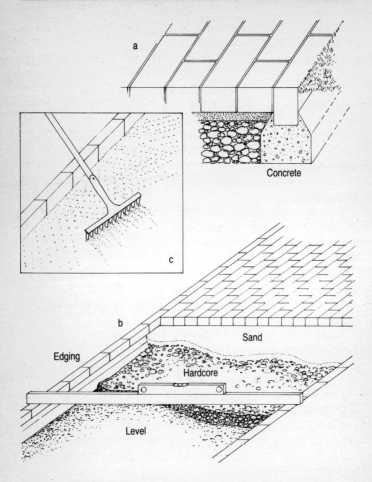

a

Concrete

c

b

Sand

Edging

Hardcore

Level

FIG. 14 (a) *Brick on edge or kerbing, in concrete, makes the edging. Mark the area with pegs, check the corners with a square, and horizontals with a spirit level. (b) Ram in hardcore, with sand to fill any voids, and a flat layer of sand on which the paviors are set. Raking gets the sand to an even level.*

put on the polythene – the level of sand underneath is to prevent the polythene tearing on lumps in the aggregate – and cover that with 50 mm or so (2–3 in) of builders' sand.

Tamp that down level. Put in your edging, to keep everything in the one place. Let it set firmly. Now you have an enclosed space, with a sand base on which to lay your bricks (Figure 14), or paviors, in whatever pattern you decide. It can be simple stretcher bond, with an appropriate number of half bricks making up the spaces. It can be herringbone, parquet, or whatever.

You will have bricks touching at the edges. No need for any 10 mm mortar gap here. The small gaps that are left are filled in with a dryish mix of sand and mortar. Water it in lightly, not to flood the material out again. Clean off any brickwork that has this mortar mix on it, using a damp cloth or a rag. Leave overnight to set: check next day and everything should be firm and stable.

Paviors are best laid with a plate vibrator (Figure 15) to level the surface. This machine can be hired, but you have to ensure you work with edges to the driveway that are firm and well set. Otherwise, the vibrator moves everything out of place and you have to start all over again.

The main requirements are for a drive that will stand up to normal household traffic, will not sprout weeds every five minutes, and will not be slippery in wet or icy weather.

You have, of course, to be able to get into an existing garage – that means the levels at the end of the drive and the entry to the garage have to balance. Your edges have to be at the same level as the rest of the drive. If there is to be any camber – a slight slope over the surface – then make it one where the middle is very slightly higher than the sides. That lets rain run off. It is

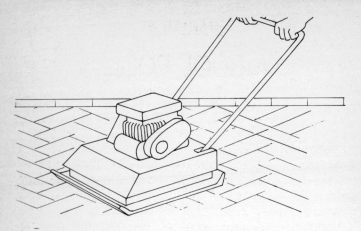

FIG. 15 Items like this plate vibrator are worth hiring. They make an excellent job of firming up paths, patios and driveways. Just be sure your edging has set firmly before using one of these machines, however.

also easier for clearing snow or autumn leaves.

Make sure you are not working over essential drains, or services like gas or electricity. If so, check the utilities concerned first. At the very least, make a permanent note of which services go where, in case you need access at some future date.

Materials and equipment required: bricks/paviors, sand, cement, mixing board, aggregates, float, buckets, shovels, water. Pegs, club hammer, bolster, safety goggles. Spirit level, straight-edge. Plate vibrator. Old clothes, gloves.

CHAPTER 8

A COOL POOL

A garden pool has a calming influence. That helps to explain the growing popularity of water features, as they are called nowadays – ponds, pools, fountains and waterfalls mainly.

Manufacturers have seen the growing market and responded by bringing out pre-formed liners for pools, pre-cast ponds and pools, kits for fountains and waterfalls. There are low-voltage lighting systems that can be incorporated, even underwater.

Be safe: With electricity, it is essential to have items checked out – and preferably fitted – by a competent electrician. Power and water are bad mixers.

We are going to be looking at some of the simpler situations: putting a pond or pool where none already exists, and modifying an existing water feature.

LINING A POOL

Using a liner to form a pool or pond is probably the simplest method. It means a water feature can be created anywhere, and typically in the middle of a large lawn. That's where we will make our one. And we'll have an edging of brick, with a brick pathway leading to it.

The process is the normal one we have used before. See the design first; put it on paper; have a dry run.

Then go ahead. Materials are fairly straightforward. A hosepipe can set out the shape we want. That lets us dig out the space, to a suitable depth, perhaps giving a split-level effect. It's no harder to do than one big hole. Go 200–300 mm (8–12 in) deep, for example, leave a 225 mm (9 in) shelf, and dig in the middle to a further 200–300 mm (8–12 in). Stones, rocks, roots and anything that could puncture the lining have to be removed, of course.

If you keep the sides at a slope, this helps to prevent the sides from falling in, particularly in light soils. The actual floor, or floors, should be compacted by treading all over them: just be careful around the edges, not to make them crumble in.

Assuming all the stones and so on have been removed, you could simply put in the liner. Adding a layer of sand first, however, is a better idea that makes sure there is a smooth, stable bed for the liner. If there is very stony ground, then a polyester mat is available from most garden centres as a cushion for the liner.

CHECK SIZES

But what size of liner do we need anyway? Your local water garden centre may be able to advise you, but try this calculation first, to see how it works out. The size of polythene or synthetic rubber lining you need is about twice the depth of the pond at its deepest part, added to the maximum length and also to the maximum width. (That's the maximum length plus twice the depth, multiplied by the maximum width plus twice the depth.)

Drape the liner over the surface you have dug out, placing some bricks on the edges to keep it in place. Turn on the hose and fill the pool, slowly. The weight of water will make the liner take up the given shape. Creases can be swept out with a broom, to make a tidier finish, but don't worry unduly about inevitable small lines that are left. Fill the pool to about 50 mm (2 in) from the ground level, making sure the retaining bricks are not pulled in and that there is enough material to do the job properly.

Now trim the extra material, leaving a good margin – 300 mm (12 in) minimum. Trim with brick edging, or better still with a brick pathway bedded on mortar a bit stiffer than usual, and joints filled with a dryish mix of cement and sand, lightly watered in. The idea is to have an attractive edging strong enough to keep the extra pool liner material in place, and to have a short overlap at the pool itself. About 25 mm (1 in) should be sufficient.

That's one method. But we know how to work with mortar, and with concrete, so let's think about making a concrete pool, finished with surrounding brickwork. A regular, rectangular shape is easiest to deal with here.

The site has been chosen, and does not affect any main services like gas or electricity. Now we dig down, a good spade's depth, to the shape and size we want. The foundation will be hard-core to around 75–100 mm (3–4 in), well rammed down and any spaces filled in with damp sand (this is 'blinding').

Make the sides of the pond or pool sloping inwards, from the top, to around 25°: it makes for easier working for one thing. At this stage, have a dry run with shuttering – lengths of wood that can be laid over the walls, joined at the top by other pieces of wood, to keep everything in place and let the concrete set properly.

Wire netting makes a good reinforcing material, for the base we are making and for the walls we have prepared. Cut it to size and shape, remembering that heavy gloves, and wire-cutters, will be needed.

MAKING A FLOOR

Dig out the space, and make a flat floor, with flat but sloping walls. Make up any wood shuttering you will use with the concrete. Try it for size, making sure it can all be held together. Cut the wire netting as reinforcement. Put the netting in place, on the floor and on the walls. Now comes the concreting.

The concrete will be a 1:2:4 cement:sand:aggregate mix with some waterproofing additive. The floor of the pool or pond is done first, to a depth of around 100 mm (4 in). The walls follow, to the chosen depth. If it is possible, try to do floor and walls at the same time. Joining up areas of concrete can be a bit awkward sometimes.

It will often help to have shuttering – stretches of wood – to retain the wall, and this is another reason why a sloping wall is helpful: it keeps the concrete from 'running away'. It helps to have a uniform depth of concrete over all four walls.

Leave things to start the curing process overnight. Once it is set, fill the pool with water – concrete can still absorb some water at this stage. After a few days, drain off this water and allow four or five days for hardening of the concrete.

With a dilute solution of PVA adhesive brushed on first, you can apply a 25 mm (1 in) layer of rendering, in a 1:3 cement:soft sand mix which contains waterproofing additive as recommended by the manufacturer.

Take a short break if you wish, and then it will be time to continue with the edging. Bricks can be used simply as a single layer of edging, but considering the work you have already put in, a pathway is the thing to go for.

PATTERNS

Try a pattern of two bricks, side by side, as the width of the path. The next row will be one brick in the middle with a half-brick either side of that. And so on, to the corner, or to an adjoining pathway, patio, retaining wall or whatever feature already exists in the garden.

An alternative could be bricks laid end to end as far as is required, with a simple bond outside that, using a half brick as necessary, another end-to-end layer, and so on, perhaps to four bricks deep. It looks like a wall lying flat, in stretcher bond.

The widths are entirely a matter of taste, and of available space. In effect, you are making a small path (see Chapter 6). That means you need to have the surrounding soil or grass removed from the edges of the pool or pond-to-be.

Lay your path in an appropriate mortar mix, and bed in as normal. A dryish mortar-cement mix is suitable for the surface, lightly watered in.

Concrete is alkaline, and your pool or pond will have to be conditioned before anything goes in, particularly fish. Proprietary compounds are available, which will neutralize the lime and improve the concrete finish by 'sealing' the surface. Leave a few more days before putting any fish in. It is better to err on the side of caution here, and even then try one or two fish at a time, just to make sure they stay healthy.

If you get leaks at any time, you will have the choice of using a sealing compound, as directed by the manufacturer, or of using a flexible liner. Largish cracks – 10 mm (3/8 in) or more – will need to be filled with mortar first, before repairs are carried out with compound or a lining.

This is a project where it is important to have materials that are in suitable colour and texture, to match up with existing items such as walls or a patio.

There is no point in rushing with this kind of project: it takes time, and money, and patience. Do it in your mind's eye first, draw it up on paper, and then have a dry run with the materials before anything else.

A RAISED POOL

Raised pools are good, to make a feature in their own right, or simply to make it easier for a handicapped person to sit at the side and enjoy the garden like everyone else.

A pool which is raised has other advantages over one which is sunk into the ground. It is easier to build up the edging round the pre-formed rigid liner than to dig a hole.

Having selected a suitable former, to suit the space available, you will have to set this rigid material on a firm, probably compacted, and level base. Mark round the perimeter. Make a strip foundation on this perimeter, for your brick wall.

No more than nine courses of brickwork should be needed. If it is going much above this, consider sinking the liner partly into the ground, again on a firm, compacted, level base.

The liner itself needs something to sit on, and 150 mm (6 in) of sand is suitable. This will hold things steady. Then back-fill with suitable material, to hold the pool really firm. A small gap between the edge of the liner material and your wall is covered with bricks – side by side gives a good, firm edge, allowing an overlap on the pool of perhaps 25 mm (1 in). It is like making a large-scale planter, but putting in a pool instead of plants (Figure 16).

You need to decide where it will go, what type or style of bricks will be most suitable to blend in with the existing scene, and whether you are making this a focal

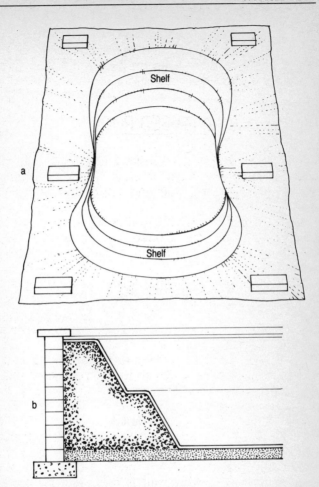

FIG. 16 *Pools can have flexible or rigid liners.* (a) *Flexible liners usually provide a bottom, a wide shelf, and then an edging all round. Bricks keep the liner in place.* (b) *A rigid liner, on a base of sand, with a brick retaining wall, the space back-filled with soil.*

point in its own right or including it, say, into a rockery. The same points are applicable: decide the situation, create a retaining shape, place the rigid liner on a bed of sand that is level and firm, fill in with soil or suitable material, and cover the edge with bricks to form a slight overlap.

It is difficult sometimes to know what to do for the best, in terms of safeguarding young children. They enjoy playing at a pool or pond, but cannot always be supervised full-time. A safety element that has been suggested is to incorporate plastic garden mesh across the pond or pool, just below the water line: green mesh would not show up too badly.

This could be held in place, underneath the edging of brickwork, with a series of pegs or even hooks, as necessary.

Materials and equipment needed: flexible or rigid liner, sand, cement, aggregates, mixing board, trowel, shovels and buckets. Club hammer, bolster, safety goggles. Spade. Wood, nails. Spirit level, straight-edge. Sealant, PVA. Old clothes, gloves. Damp cloth.

CHAPTER 9

MAKING AMENDS

Nothing is ever perfect. We always want to change things, to put right things that are wrong. To add to whatever already exists. This is a short list of some things we can do, to make our garden more as we would have it be.

REPLACING DAMAGED BRICKS

Constantly exposed to the elements, masonry can deteriorate. Common problems are crumbly mortar joints that loosen bricks and make a structure dangerous.

Damaged bricks can be replaced (Figure 17). However, don't attempt to replace more than about 10 bricks without propping up the rest of the masonry.

Drill a row of closely-spaced holes in the mortar joints surrounding the damaged brick. Use a 10 mm (⅜ in) diameter masonry bit in an electric drill. Hack out the weakened mortar with a cold chisel and a club hammer. Lever out the brick with a bolster chisel. If need be, drill into the brick.

Clean around the hole and brush out dust and debris. Dampen inside the hole so the bricks won't suck the water out of the repair mortar too quickly and cause it to crack. Mix up some dry-mix mortar, then trowel a 10 mm (⅜ in) bed on to the base of the hole. Scrape some mortar up one side of the hole.

Butter the top and one end of the replacement brick.

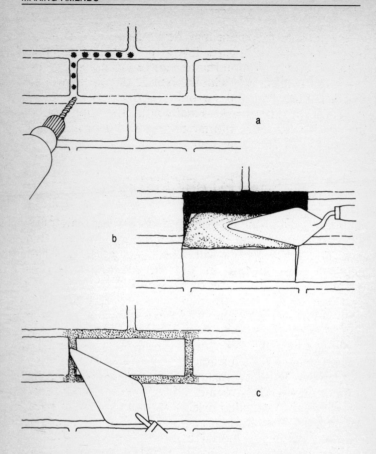

FIG. 17 (a) *If a cold chisel won't do, use an electric drill –
10 mm (³/₈ in) masonry bit – to drill the mortar joints around
a damaged brick. Chop out the mortar – a bolster helps with
large bits. Clean up the hole with a brush – don't use your
hands, bricks are rough – and dampen the masonry.* (b)
*Spread mortar on the base of the hole and one end. Butter the
top and the other end of a replacement brick and tap it in.* (c)
Point up to follow the existing profile.

A matching replacement may be obtained in a demolition site or builder's yard. Insert the brick in the hole, buttered end to non-mortared end of the hole. Tap the brick gently into place with the handle of your trowel so that it is flush with the surrounding masonry.

Repeat for other bricks. Finally point the joint around the brick with more mortar to match the profile with that of the surrounding wall.

SPALLED BRICKWORK

Old bricks are prone to spalling, where water penetrates the faces, freezes and breaks off the outer surface. This not only looks ugly but will soon disintegrate. It is like neglecting woodwork in the house, or outside – dangerous, and has to be dealt with.

Where a brick is badly spalled, replace it. If it is only slightly damaged a repair can be made. Mix up some mortar with a proprietary cement colouring powder, added according to the instructions. If you can't obtain a suitable match, try substituting brick dust.

Brush away loose material and paint on a strong solution of PVA adhesive and water. Hold a length of thin wood below the spalled brick to protect it from smears, and trowel the mortar over the primed surface. Carefully shape the mortar to resemble the profiles of the other bricks and leave to set. The repair will be darker looking at first but will dry out lighter.

POINTING BRICKWORK

Mortar joints are usually shaped to deflect rainwater. To prepare a wall for repointing, rake out the joint to about 10 mm (⅜ in) with a chisel or suitable piece of metal.

Brush out the dirt and debris. Wet the joints and refill with new mortar. Pointing mortar is available in bags dry-mixed: just add water.

Starting with the horizontal joints, press the blade of the trowel on to the mortar and angle it inwards at the top. Slide the trowel downwards off the brick below to form a neat V-shape. Angle the vertical joints either way.

CLEANING OLD BRICKS

If may be possible to get cheap bricks if you offer to collect old ones, and then clean them yourself. Cement and sand mortar will be difficult to remove and a brick hammer will be needed. This has a square face and a long curved blade and a chisel end, or it can have detachable combs or serrated blades which fit into the end.

TRY CLEAN WATER

If you think existing brickwork is looking a bit dingy, don't rush in with a paintbrush – try cleaning the bricks with a hard-bristled brush and clean water. Do not use soap; it can stain the surface.

And if the discolouring is caused by some kind of mould, then you need to clean it up with a fungicide. Apply as directed by the manufacturer's instructions, leave for about a week, and brush off the dead mould. Then try masonry primer or stabilizing fluid, again as directed.

PAINTING BRICKWORK

Painting brickwork, new brickwork anyway, is not a very good idea. It spoils the appearance and the paint, once it is on, is difficult to remove completely.

If you have decided that a coat of paint is called for, to brighten up the place or just because you want to, then put on a coat of stabilizing fluid or masonry primer first. The paint should be exterior-grade masonry emulsion. Paint in sections, starting from the top. If the wall still shines through like a brown ghost, after this coat has dried, put on another.

Some people like a paint roller, but it is not as efficient as a brush when it comes to reaching into corners and crevices. Newspaper spread under the wall, or wherever you are working, may well save a lot of time in cleaning up the adjoining surfaces also.

WHITE STAINS

The white stain sometimes encountered on outside walls, giving a powdery, salt-like surface, is known as efflorescence. Salts rise to the surface as the material dries out. There is no point in trying to paint over this with emulsion. Nor will it simply wash off. Regular cleaning with a stiff-bristled brush will help. An alternative is to try your local builders' merchant, and ask for chemical masonry cleaner. Explain the problem, and read the instructions carefully.

Once the wall is thoroughly dry, the efflorescence should disappear. And if you still want to paint this particular brickwork, ask at the merchant's for suitable alkali-resisting primer before using an oil-based paint. You may be advised to try silicone-based water repellant, to keep out damp.

Stains on paths can often be dealt with. Garden centres, DIY stores, and motor accessory shops all have a wide range of removers nowadays. Indicate whether the problem is caused by oil, grease, rust, moss or anything else. With fresh oil, you may find cat litter a good absorbent in an emergency.

KERBING

Damaged kerbing need present no problem. Loosen the damaged length of kerbing with a club hammer, and prise it out with a spade. Dig out 50 mm (1 in) of sub-base below, and ram the surface down with a stout piece of timber.

Mix bedding mortar from a sand-cement ready-mix, to a dryish constituency, and spread it in the gap. Damp the new piece of kerbstone and tap it down, protecting the face with a piece of wood. Check levels and let it dry properly.

ADD-ONS

Where a wall has some broken or loose bricks, it may be an idea to put up some baskets or planters while you are at it. Remove the loose brick, and set in one or more pieces of mild steel to act as shelf supports. When firmly set, they can take small baskets or planters.

There is no reason why a number of these supports could not take a window box, transposed to a sunnier setting, for example. Window boxes aren't restricted to being under windows!

An alternative, on an existing wall with no holes, is to add on a hanging bracket, with screws plugged into the mortar and allowed to set. Vine eyes can take support wire (Figure 18).

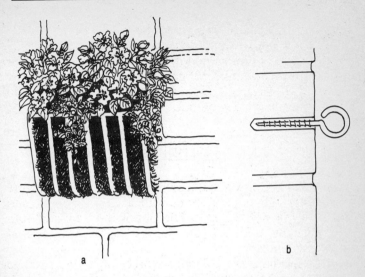

FIG. 18 *If you have a wall with loose bricks, instead of simply replacing them, try adding something on – some fancy wall baskets, or a window box or two. (b) Vine eyes make for easy use of wire. Trellis can be kept up this way also.*

And another possibility is to put up trellis, with a packing piece of wood behind, to take the screws, and also to leave a gap for plants to climb through.

If you have the patience to put the trellis on hinges, the whole thing can be taken away from the wall should any later repairs become necessary.

Materials and equipment required: use materials indicated for specific work. In any case, you'll need old clothes, a pair of gloves, cleaning fluid like white spirit for the brush and/or roller. Safety goggles should be used to prevent splashing in the eyes.

CHAPTER 10

DREAM GARDENS

This is not a chapter of work to be done: it's for sitting back, and dreaming. Now that we know we can cope with brickwork, make up mortar and concrete, carry out some projects for ourselves, we want to look ahead.

Maybe we've always hankered after a splendidly arched gateway, leading to a secret garden. Maybe all we ever wanted to do was find out how to make a decent base for that greenhouse we promised ourselves.

That, in fact, is what we are doing in this concluding chapter of events. We're looking at projects still to come, seeing what they look like, seeing how they will fit in with our needs, and our dreams.

AN ARCHWAY

Arches always look splendid, but they take time and care. Draw up the design on paper first and see how it works in practice. Two walls, for example make a gateway. The arch goes over the top. But it needs something to hold it up.

That's where a former comes in. This is a wooden template, typically of 100 mm × 50 mm (4 in × 2 in) section, with 3 mm (1/8 in) plywood over that. Figure 19 shows the idea including a wooden frame with supporting legs. Note that you can add a circular piece of ply to the front and back to make sure the framework is strong enough and retains its shape.

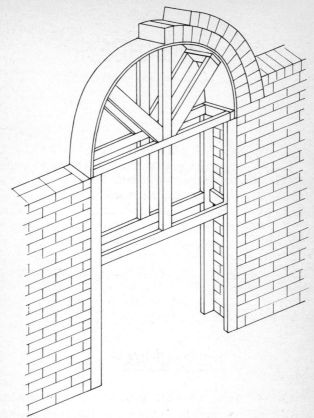

FIG. 19 *Now it's time to dream . . . of gateways with splendid arches.*

You can have a dry run with this template on the ground. Make the arch itself with stretcher or header faces showing. Showing stretcher faces will mean fairly wide joints on the outer edge – trying to cut bricks into wedge shapes is tricky. Header bricks, one or two courses, give a better look and would fit in with a full-brick wall.

THAT GREENHOUSE

For your long-awaited greenhouse, you need to start with the plan detailed on paper. It will need electricity for lighting, heating, propagating, mist culture – all the goodies.

At this stage, we're really only looking ahead, and thinking about it. But we know what is needed in terms of foundation work at least. This is really going right back to the beginning, of course, ready to start again.

Mark the edge of each side of the foundation strip, using string lines and profile boards. Remove the top soil and put in marker pegs at about 1 m (3 ft 3 in) intervals. Their tops show where the concrete surface goes – level with a hard surface or 25–50 mm (1–2 in) below a lawn edge.

Check levels. Dig a trench to the required width and depth. With soft soil, dig a little deeper.

Fill the trench with hard-core rammed down, and 'blinded' with sand to leave no gaps. Mix concrete and shovel it into the trench, making sure it is well bedded down. Remove any air, by tamping the surface. Remove marker pegs and fill gaps with concrete. Let the concrete cure thoroughly.

Fit string lines on the profile broads to outline wall edges. Lay a mortar base, and build up the walls in courses.

It may be only a dream at this stage, but this is the kind of work we can look ahead to doing now. There's more to come? Certainly. This is not the end. This is a beginning.

INDEX

Page numbers in *italic* refer to the illustrations